Travel Through
China

Lynn Huggins-Cooper

Teacher Created Resources

Copyright © 2007 QEB Publishing

First published in the United States by
QEB Publishing, Inc.
23062 La Cadena Drive
Laguna Hills, CA 92653

This edition published by
Teacher Created Resources, Inc.
6421 Industry Way
Westminster, CA 92683

www.teachercreated.com

Library of Congress Control Number: 2007000945

ISBN 978 1 4206 8280 9

Written by Lynn Huggins-Cooper
Designed by Rahul Dhiman (Q2A Media)
Editor Honor Head
Picture Researcher Pritika Ghura (Q2A Media)

Publisher Steve Evans
Creative Director Zeta Davies
Senior Editor Hannah Ray

Printed and bound in China

Picture credits

Key: t = top, b = bottom, m = middle, l = left, r = right, FC = front cover

Dimitrios Kaisaris/ **Shutterstock**: 4t, **Index Stock Imagery**/ **Photolibrary**: 4, 12t, 19t, tamir niv/
Shutterstock: 6, **Photomediacom**/ **Shutterstock**: 7t, wu xiao bai/ **Shutterstock**: 7b, **Nordic
Photos**/ **Photolibrary**: 8, Ray Laskowitz/ **Lonely Planet Images**: 9t, Chris Mellor/ **Lonely Planet
Images**: 9m, Bruce B/ **Lonely Planet Images**: 10, **Imagestate Ltd**/ **Photolibrary**: 11t, **Photonica
Inc**/ **Photolibrary**: 11b, 15b, Nicholas Pavloff/ **Lonely Planet Images**: 12b, Bill Wassman/ **Lonely
Planet Images**: 13t, Gautier Willaume/ **Istockphoto**: 13m, Greg Elms/ **Lonely Planet Images**:
14t, Paul Barton/**Corbis**: 14b, Phil Weymouth/ **Lonely Planet Images**: 15t, Diana Mayfield/ **Lonely
Planet Images**: 16b, Richard I'Anson/ **Lonely Planet Images**: 16–17t, Lee Foster/ **Lonely Planet
Images**: 17b, Chinatiger/ **Bigstockphoto**: 18, Gergely Bényi/ **Shutterstock**: 19b, Hsin Chu, Taiwan:
20t, **Photo Researchers, Inc.**/ **Photolibrary**: 20b, Craig Pershouse/ **Lonely Planet Images**: 22b,
Jon Arnold Images/ **Photolibrary**: 23t, **Panorama Media (Beijing) Ltd**/ **Photolibrary**: 23m, 27b,
Garry Weare/ **Lonely Planet Images**: 24b, **Peter Arnold Images Inc**/ **Photolibrary**: 25t, **Animals
Animals** / **Earth Scenes**/ **Photolibrary**: 25b, 27t, Keren Su/ **Lonely Planet Images**: 26b.

Words in **bold** can be found in the glossary on page 31.

Contents

Where in the world is China?

China is a huge country, divided up into areas called **provinces**. It covers most of east Asia, and it is the fourth-largest country in the world. As it is so large, it has many different **climates**, from **temperate** to **subarctic**. China is home to people of 56 different **ethnic groups**. Han is the largest group, making up around 85% of the **population**.

One in five of all the people in the world live in China. The population is growing by an incredible 15 million people each year. The government introduced a "one child" policy in 1979 so that people did not have large families, which would add to the overpopulation problem.

China includes Hong Kong, which Britain handed back to the People's Republic of China in 1997. Hong Kong is quite different from the rest of China. It is very westernized as a result of having been part of Britain for more than 150 years.

Did you know?

OFFICIAL NAME: People's Republic of China

SURROUNDING COUNTRIES: Russia, India, Afghanistan, Bhutan, Myanmar, Kazakhstan, North Korea, Kyrgyzstan, Laos, Macau, Mongolia, Nepal, Pakistan, Tajikistan, and Vietnam

SURROUNDING SEAS AND OCEANS: Pacific Ocean, South China Sea

CAPITAL: Beijing

AREA: 3,705,407 sq. mi. (9,596,960 sq. km)

POPULATION: 1,303,701,000

LIFE EXPECTANCY: 71 years

RELIGIONS: Taoism, Buddhism, Islam

LANGUAGES: Chinese (Mandarin), Cantonese

CLIMATE: ranges from desert to **tropical** to subarctic

HIGHEST MOUNTAIN: Mount Everest in the Himalayas (29,035 ft./8,850 m high).

MAJOR RIVERS: Yangtze River (3,964 mi./6,380 km long), the Huang He River (3,393 mi./ 5,460 km long)

CURRENCY: yuan

What is China like?

There are many different landscapes throughout China. There are hills, **plains**, and **river deltas** in the east and deserts, high **plateaus,** and mountains in the west.

Deadly desert

The Taklimakan desert in the west of China is the second-largest desert in the world. It is known as the "desert of death" because it is so dry. The Gobi desert is also in China and southern Mongolia. The grains of sand in the Gobi desert are smooth and round, unlike typical sand, which is coarse and irregular. In very dry weather conditions, the sand slides down the dunes and the grains bump together making a booming noise, like spooky music!

Legend has it that the Gobi desert was created when a magical Mongolian chief was being chased by the Chinese army. He cast a spell and the land behind him died, leaving the desert.

In summer, the temperature in the Gobi desert rises to a blistering 135°F (57°C), and in winter, temperatures can drop to -76°F (-60°C).

Varied climate

The climate in China is very varied. In Hainan, in the south, they have warm, tropical weather and you only need light clothes. In Manchuria, in the north, you need warm clothes because the climate is subarctic. This means the temperatures are very low, as low as -22°F (-30°C) in the winter, and the summers are short and warm.

Hainan province is famous for its stunning scenery and beautiful beaches. Tianya Haijiao and Dadonghai are two well-known beaches and many people visit every year to sunbathe and to swim in the ocean.

Where people live

Although China has many big, busy cities, 70% of the people live in **rural** areas. This is because people prefer to settle and live where the climate is mild and food crops can be grown. Shandong province is on the east coast and its climate is very mild. About 91 million people live there because the weather is so pleasant.

The huge Mount Everest is on the border between China and Nepal.

Getting around

In the past, rickshaws were used to carry rich and important people through the streets of China. Today they are used by tourists.

China has many airports and a good system of internal flights, which makes traveling across the huge country much quicker. Many people also travel by car. Large cities such as Shanghai and Beijing have big highways, but there are lots of cars, and traffic jams are often a problem. The traffic also causes high levels of air pollution. It can make traveling unpleasant and some people wear anti-pollution masks when they travel.

There are many fast, busy roads in China, but they are often clogged with traffic. There are around 15,000,000 cars in China.

Traveling by train

The larger Chinese cities have underground railways, which are very busy. They have special guards to squash people into the cars during rush hour. But the underground trains are still a great way to get around quickly and to avoid the traffic jams. China also has a large rail network above ground, with **sleeper cars** for long-distance travel.

On your bike!

Bicycles are very popular in China. There are 300 million bikes whizzing about the country. Pedicabs are bikes with a passenger seat attached and these are used like taxis. There are also a few tourist rickshaws and sedan chairs. Rickshaws are small carts pulled by one person. A sedan chair is a compartment in which a person sits. The chair is then lifted up and carried by two people, one at either end.

YOU'VE GOT MAIL

Today, I went on a boat trip on a **junk** and visited the floating homes and shops in Hong Kong—what a way to travel! We went to a place called Aberdeen, which is an area of the harbor crammed with junks and **sampans**. About 6,000 people live and work there. I bought a **jade** charm, which is very pretty, and some noodles for lunch —yum!
Su Ling

Many people in China travel by bike. There are up to 10 million bicycles in Beijing alone!

Major cities

China has many beautiful cities that contain an interesting mix of ancient monuments and modern buildings.

Beautiful Beijing

Beijing is the capital of the People's Republic of China. After Shanghai, it is the city with the second-largest population in China. The Forbidden City (or Forbidden Palace) at the center of Beijing is a beautiful place that you can visit. It used to be the Imperial Palace, where the **emperors** who used to rule China lived, and is now a huge museum. It is listed by **UNESCO** as the largest collection of ancient wooden buildings in the world and it is a **World Heritage site**.

The Forbidden City has 800 buildings and more than 8,000 rooms.

Skyscraping city

Shanghai is on the banks of the Yangtze River Delta in eastern China. It is China's largest city and the eighth-largest city in the world. There are many modern skyscrapers in Shanghai. The Oriental Pearl Tower is 1,535 ft. (468 m) tall and visitors can climb to the top to look at the views. There is a revolving restaurant, a science museum, and a disco room as you travel up the tower.

Shanghai is a beautiful waterfront city. It is one of the world's busiest ports and became the largest cargo port in the world in 2005.

Hi! I went to Shanghai with Mom for a visit last week. It was the first time we've been. We went to the People's Park one morning and saw hundreds of people doing Tai Chi—a series of movements and exercises. Afterward, we went to the Oriental Pearl Tower and had lunch in the revolving restaurant. The views were amazing! Then we did some shopping. We went to the Xiangyang market, which is a great place to buy clothes, and then to Dongtai Lu market to buy some ornaments as presents. Mom spent hours looking at the antiques.

Love,
Shushi

Many people practice Tai Chi to keep their bodies and minds strong and healthy.

Farming in China

Farming is very important in China. About two-thirds of the working population of China work in **agriculture** or with **livestock**. As you travel across China, you will see vast areas of farmland. China is the world's largest producer of rice, wheat, **soy beans,** and cane sugar. It **exports** many of these products around the world and you can buy them in supermarkets as well as specialty shops.

This woman has to carry heavy buckets to water her crops.

There are about 12 million yaks in China. They are used for milk, meat, and their skins.

Fishermen catch fish to eat and sell. Fish is a very popular food in China.

Best crops

Rice is a major crop in China. It is grown in fields that are flooded and drained to help the rice grow. Water from rivers and streams is piped into the fields. Cotton and oilseeds are also widely grown, especially as **cash crops** for export. China has many mouths to feed and it is **self-sufficient** in cereal, fish, and meat.

The fields in which rice is grown are called paddy fields.

My mom is a rice farmer. She has learned how to grow better rice, in easier ways, from the Agricultural Broadcasting School. The school uses TV, audio and video recordings, and computer programs to teach people who are scattered all over our huge country. Going to a college is hard for many people because they live far away and cannot leave their fields to travel to study. The Agricultural Broadcasting School helps everyone learn at home. Now my mom is growing new types of rice that are specially suited to our conditions. This will make it easier to grow good crops and means that our village will have plenty of rice to sell. My mom runs training classes for other farmers when they are not busy growing rice—so, now everybody is learning.

Yin

Food and drink

In China, a lot of food is cooked in a wok, a special pan which is rounded rather than flat. It is used for stir-frying food such as noodles, bean sprouts, and bamboo shoots. Stir-frying makes the food cook quickly and seals in vitamins. Food is also often steamed in special bamboo baskets.

Wontons are small dough parcels containing meat or vegetables. They are often served with soup.

This family is enjoying a meal of noodles. They are eating with chopsticks.

Tea is very popular in China. It can be bought in tea shops and from special sellers in the street.

Woks can also be used for making stews and soups, as well as for stir-frying.

Something special

Different parts of China have different specialty dishes. Beijing is famous for roast duck, while Sichuan province is famous for food cooked with spices such as ginger, chilli, and star anise. The city of Xi'an is famous for its dumplings, called *jiaozi*. There are many types and each type has a different shape, depending on what is inside. Fillings include chicken and pork. Cantonese food, from the area around Guangzhou, is mildly spiced. It often includes fish and has a delicate flavor. Eastern-style food often includes fish, with dishes such as fish tail stew, hot-and-sour fish soup, steamed crabs, and deep-fried fish with bamboo shoots.

Bowl and chopsticks

Food is often eaten from small bowls using chopsticks, which even small children are able to use. Travelers sometimes find it quite difficult to use chopsticks properly because it takes practice!

It was my birthday yesterday, and Mom took me and some of my friends out for a special meal. I had a vegetarian banquet and it was so delicious, I wish my tummy held more! I had sweetcorn soup with seaweed, then deep-fried **tofu** with black bean sauce and fried rice. I had **lychees** for dessert. Lychees are my favorite, but they look like eyeballs! I had jasmine tea at the end of the meal, which smelled wonderful—and tasted pretty good, too. Have you ever tried jasmine tea?
Love,
Huo

Famous sites

China has many beautiful, historic sites to visit. Some of them are many centuries old.

The pagoda forest

A pagoda is a temple shaped like a tall tower. There is a "pagoda forest" at the Shaolin Temple in Henan province, where 220 brick and stone pagodas have been built as tombs for the monks and abbots of the temple. As you travel through the "forest," you can see many **kung fu** masters and students demonstrating their skills to visitors.

Wonder wall

The Great Wall of China was built from the 5th century B.C.E. to protect China from invasion from the fierce **nomadic** tribes of neighboring Mongolia. It is 3,977 mi. (6,400 km) long, and runs from the Shanhai Pass in the east to Lop Nur in the west.

The wall is built in very steep steps, and tourists get very tired trying to climb them!

Pagodas are sometimes made of wood, as well as from stone.

Temple visits

In Qufu, in Shandong province, many tourists visit the Temple of Confucius, named after a famous teacher and thinker. The temple is made up of many buildings, and includes nine courtyards. There are 466 rooms and 54 gateways.

Today, I visited the Great Wall. I saw one of the special forts built into the Wall and went inside. There are holes built into the wall that are about 12 in. (30 cm) high. They were used to shoot arrows from when the wall was attacked. The wall was so long—it stretched away into the distance as far as I could see. A notice said that the wall is the largest structure ever built by people.

Chang

The clay figures are very lifelike. They are different heights and have hairstyles according to the rank of soldier they represent.

Clay army

In March 1974, farmers drilling a well to the east of Mount Lishan in Shaanxi province unearthed the **necropolis** of the Emperor Qin Shi Huang and found the first of what would eventually be nearly 9,000 life-size **terracotta** warriors. This incredible army of red clay soldiers was created to guard the emperor in death. Each warrior was given a real weapon, such as a crossbow, spear, or sword. Today, you can visit these warriors in the Museum of Qin Terracotta Warriors at Xi'an.

Art in China

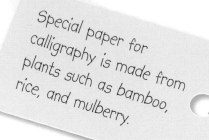

Special paper for calligraphy is made from plants such as bamboo, rice, and mulberry.

China has many different types of traditional art, including silk painting, calligraphy, and embroidery. Chinese art is impressive and often highly detailed.

Beautiful writing

Chinese calligraphy is a very beautiful way of writing that has been done for thousands of years. It uses special solid blocks of ink, made from soot or oil smoke mixed with water. The writing is done with brushes, like a painting.

Sing a story

Chinese opera tells the stories of heroes and supernatural creatures. The actors have their faces painted with bright colors to make their features look bigger. Visitors can buy masks of the painted faces, which can be used as ornaments.

Paper decorations

Paper was invented in China in the 1st century C.E. Paper cuts are a traditional Chinese decoration. Using scissors or a special knife, an artist cuts a complicated picture of plants, animals, or people into paper.

Paper cuts are used to decorate houses during festivals and holidays.

I went to a kite festival yesterday! The sky was full of colorful kites in different shapes and designs. There were butterflies, birds, dragonflies, goldfish, and even huge dragons. A Nantong whistle kite swooped right past my head! It shrieked really loudly. All the amazing kites I saw are made from thin bamboo sticks and silk or paper. Kite builders have to master "the four skills". That's making the frame, pasting on the silk, painting the silk, and then flying the kite!

Mei

Embroidery and silk

Chinese embroidery usually shows pictures of beautiful women, dragons, and cherry blossoms. It has been created in China for centuries and tourists often buy embroidered objects to take home as souvenirs. Silk painting is also traditional in China and is used on screens, fans, kits, and clothing.

A kite's bamboo frame has to be completely symmetrical so that the kite is evenly balanced. Then, the silk is hand painted.

Chinese exports

China **manufactures** many different types of goods, which it exports all over the world. If you like playing computer or console games, it is likely that you have played some games that were made in China. Many games and toys come from Hong Kong. It is amazing to think how far your toys may have traveled before you play with them! China is famous for exporting many other things, too.

Silk road

Hundreds of years ago, long lines of carts traveled through Asia to other countries selling silk. The route they took was called the Silk Road. Today, many types of silk are still exported from China. If you visit China, you will see lots of brightly colored silk clothing for sale.

Pearl place

China produces more pearls than any other country. Most of China's freshwater pearl farms are near the Yangtze River and are within 310 mi. (500 km) of Shanghai. Most of the pearls are made into jewelry, but some are crushed and made into medicine or cosmetics.

Silk has been used to create these traditional-style Chinese costumes.

YOU'VE GOT MAIL

My dad bought me a beautiful pearl bracelet for my birthday yesterday. Pearls are very cheap in China. Dad said he visited the pearl farm and saw the shellfish, called mussels, that are used to grow the pearls. The farmer puts a grain in the mussel. The grain scratches the mussel, so the mussel makes layers of material to cover the grain and stop it from scratching. The layers build up and a pearl is made. The mussels were in special ponds, with ducks, too, so the farmer had two ways to make money —pearls and ducks!

Ting

Printing books

China has huge factories that print books in many different languages. Book companies from around the world send their books to China to be printed, where it is much cheaper.

Books are printed onto very long sheets of paper and then sliced up into sections to make pages.

Festivals and holidays

In China, there are many festivals and holidays. These are also celebrated by Chinese people who live in other countries around the world.

Happy New Year!

In late January or early February, Chinese New Year parties fill the streets with parades and dances. Businesses close so that everyone can join in the fun. People in lion costumes dance through the streets, bringing blessings to businesses and homes that leave out offerings for the lion. Children wake up early to find small red envelopes containing sweets or money under their pillows.

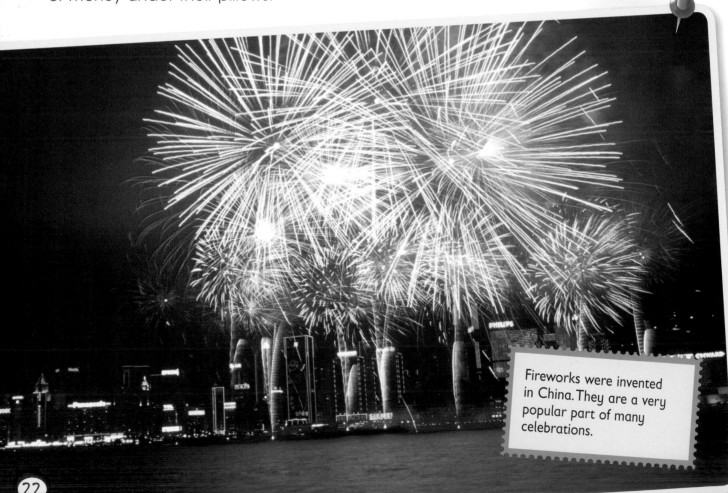

Fireworks were invented in China. They are a very popular part of many celebrations.

Before a dragon boat enters a competition, it is "brought to life" by painting eyes on the dragon's face in a special ceremony.

Lion dancers are accompanied by music played with gongs and drums. Firecrackers are set off to bring good luck.

Tuen Ng

In June, Tuen Ng, or the Dragon Boat festival, takes place all over East Asia. Wonderful boats, carved and painted to look like dragons, are raced across the water. Drums beat out a fast rhythm as the crews row the boats as quickly as they can to the finish line. A famous dragon boat race takes place every year in Hong Kong, with teams from around the world taking part. Special rice dumplings called *zongzi*, made of sticky rice wrapped in bamboo or reed leaves, are cooked and eaten during Tuen Ng.

YOU'VE GOT MAIL

My family is having a party for New Year. We are going to see the lion dances and parades, and then we are coming home to watch some fireworks and have a special meal. We are having lettuce wraps, spring rolls, and sticky cake, which is like steamed fruit cake. It will be great fun!

Love,
Cheng

The Himalayas

The Himalayan Mountains stretch 1,616 mi. (2,600 km) across southwest China, northern Pakistan, Nepal, Bhutan, and northern India. The Himalayas have been described as "where the Earth meets the sky." They are the world's highest mountain chain.

Top ten

The Himalayas contain an amazing nine of the ten highest peaks in the world. This includes Mount Everest, which is the highest mountain in the world at 29,035 ft. (8,850 m) high, and K2, which is 28,251 ft. (8,611 m) high. Both of these mountains are on the border between China and Pakistan. Any areas of the Himalayas that are above 16,010 ft. (4,880 m) have a very cold climate and are always covered in snow and ice. In the mountains, the air is very thin, which makes it hard to breathe and people get tired very quickly. Climbing expeditions take oxygen with them to avoid this.

The highest parts of the Himalayas are covered in deep snow all year round.

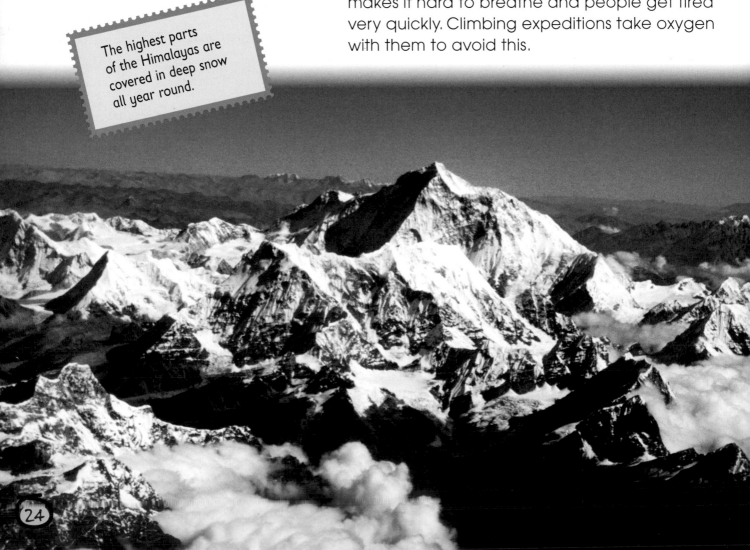

Mountain habitats

When people think of the Himalayas, they think of cold mountains, but there are many different habitats in the Himalayan range, including tropical forests and **subtropical** forests in the foothills. This means that there is a wide variety of animals and plants. Many of these animals, such as the red panda and the snow leopard, are very rare.

The red panda is also known as the *wah* because of the strange noise it makes.

Edmund Hillary and Tenzing Norgay were the first people to reach the top of Mount Everest, in 1953.

I am having a great time at Lugu Lake in the Himalayas, on the border between Sichuan province and Yannan province. The area is sometimes called "The Kingdom of Women." The Mosuo people who live there believe that women should be in charge of society and they hold all the positions of power. Mom thinks this is very sensible!
Manika

Scientists believe there may only be 35 Amur leopards left in the wild, living in China's border regions and the far east of Russia.

The environment

China is a huge country with many different landscapes and habitats, but it faces a number of environmental challenges—from poor air quality to endangered animals. However, steps are being taken to solve some of these problems.

Dust storms

The Taklimakan desert has dust storms that can carry dust all over the world. In early December 2005, there was a terrible dust storm that blew sand across China, creating many health problems, such as asthma.

Beating the storms

There is a major dust storm in China almost every year. On the outskirts of Beijing, huge forests are being planted to improve the air quality and to prevent dust from creating more health problems. The forests help put more oxygen into the air. Trees and bushes can also help stop the dust from traveling too far because they act as a barrier and stop the dust from blowing across the country.

These golden monkeys live safely in a wildlife reserve near Beijing.

China takes the protection of pandas very seriously. Until 1997, the penalty for killing a panda was execution. Today, it is 20 years imprisonment.

Save the animals

We have been fundraising this term to help save endangered animals. I have chosen to study Przewalski's Horse, or the Takhi, which is the last wild horse left in the world. The Takhi disappeared from the Gobi desert in the 1960s, but a few were still held in zoos. A breeding program has built up numbers, and the Takhi was reintroduced to the wild. There is now a herd of more than 60 horses.

Lee

Nature reserves

Many endangered animals are found in China—more than 385 threatened species according to the **IUCN Red List**. Some animals have been hunted nearly to **extinction**. Others are suffering as their habitats are destroyed by industry and building projects. China has created many nature reserves covering 289,113,296 acres (117 million hectares)—more than 12% of China—to give animals and plants a safe place to live. People are usually not allowed to build, cut down trees, or hunt on nature reserves. Protecting habitats is helping to save endangered species such as the giant panda, golden monkey, Chinese alligator, Asiatic elephant, snow leopard, and the Siberian tiger.

The Siberian tiger is the largest member of the cat family. There are only 350–450 left in the wild and some of these can be found in northeast China.

27

Activity ideas

1 Using travel brochures, cut out pictures and make a poster to show the image that China gives to tourists. What ideas and images do travel agents use to "sell" China as a holiday destination?

2 Visit a supermarket and look for food and products that have come from China. Have all the foods classified as "Chinese food," such as noodles, prawn crackers, etc. actually been made and processed in China?

3 Plan a vacation to China. Choose ten places that you would like to visit. Why did you choose those places?

4 Using books and the Internet, find out about some of the wildlife found in China and make a fact file. Create sections about different animals—anything you find interesting!

5 Imagine that you are traveling across China. Write an imaginary diary about your journey. What do you see? Who do you meet? Does anything special happen to you? What do you learn about China? You could add drawings to your diary, too.

6 Write a tourist leaflet describing a city in China. You are trying to encourage people to visit the city, so use exciting and appealing language.

7 Make a model of The Great Wall of China from papier-mâché. Before you begin, use books or the Internet to find out more about the wall.

8 Do a Web search about the floating city in Aberdeen, Hong Kong. Make notes on the information you find, and write a presentation to tell others about Aberdeen. You could print out pictures to accompany your talk.

9 Find out more about Chinese New Year. Write a report as though you spent Chinese New Year in Shanghai, and experienced it for yourself.

10 Make a dragon puppet for Chinese New Year. Concertina fold a brightly colored strip of paper—this will be your dragon's body. Make a head from a small box and tape it to the front of the body. Cut a tail out of thin cardstock, and tape it to the end of the body. Tape a craft stick to the front of your dragon, just behind and underneath its head. Tape another craft stick beneath its tail. Decorate the dragon with paint, tissue, crêpe paper, and sequins. Hold the craft sticks and make your dragon dance!

11 Find other places on the same **latitude** as China. Find out if the average temperatures are the same, or if they differ. Plot the results on a chart to compare the temperatures in the different countries.

13 Find a recipe for regional food from China— the Internet is a good source. With an adult, cook the food and eat a Chinese meal. You could also buy some examples of ready-made Chinese foods and sample them, before reviewing them and displaying the reports of the "food critics!"

NOTE FOR ADULTS:
Please ensure that children do not suffer from any food allergies before making or eating any food.

12 Make a 3-D map of China using papier-mâché. Draw the rough shape of the country on a sheet of card, and add pieces of crumpled paper, glued firmly in place, to build up the land. Don't forget the Himalayas! Coat the model in glue, and cover the whole model carefully with strips of tissue paper. Repeat this step until you have a smooth surface and leave to dry. Then paint and label your model with major cities, rivers, and mountains.

14 Make a fact file about the Terracotta Warriors —and then make a small model of a warrior from clay.

15 Carry out research using the Internet, magazines, and newspapers to find out more about the problem of dust being carried across China from the Taklimakan desert. Use your information to think of ideas to solve the problem. Can you dream up an invention that would help?

16 With an adult, visit a local Chinese supermarket and see the variety of food on offer. Compare the food in the supermarket with the food you usually eat. How is it different?

17 Find out more information on how pearls are made. Write a report about how Chinese pearls get from mussel to necklace.

18 Make a mini Chinese kite using toothpicks and tissue paper. Use the Internet or other sources to find out more about Chinese kites.

19 Try making your own paper cuts. You need a simple shape to start with. Use brightly colored paper to make your paper cut and tape it to a window when you are finished, to show it off. Search the Internet to find out more about paper cuts.

20 Make a dragon boat that floats! Using scrap bits and pieces, make a dragon boat that will float in a tub of water. It's harder than it looks because adding a dragon head and neck makes the boat "front heavy." How can you balance the weight so the boat floats in the water? Don't forget to decorate your boat!

Glossary

agriculture The production of crops or livestock

cash crop Something that is grown to sell

climate The usual weather conditions of a particular place or region

emperors Name given to the rulers of China, from 221 B.C.E. to 1912

ethnic groups A group of people who identify with each other, usually because of a shared ancestry. People within an ethnic group often speak the same language and have similar customs.

export Transporting goods to other countries

extinction When a type of animal or plant dies out completely

IUCN Red List A list of endangered species produced by the International Union for the Conservation of Nature and Natural Resources

jade A green, semiprecious gemstone

junk A traditional Chinese boat with square sails

kung fu A Chinese martial art

latitude Distance from the equator (an imaginary circle around the middle of Earth, shown on most maps)

livestock Farmed animals such as sheep, goats, and cows

lychees A fruit with sweet, white flesh and a rough, pink skin

manufacture To make or create

necropolis A prehistoric or historic burial ground or cemetery

nomadic Traveling from place to place

plains Flat, open areas of land

plateaus High flat areas of land

population The number of people who live in a particular place

provinces Districts or regions within a country

river deltas Flat plains at the mouth of a river

rural In the countryside

sampans Traditional Chinese boats with a flat bottom and oars

self-sufficient Able to provide totally for itself

sleeper cars Cars on trains for sleeping in on long journeys

soy beans A type of pulse used in cooking

subarctic The region immediately south of the Arctic Circle

subtropical Nearly tropical

temperate Weather that is not too hot nor too cold

terracotta Red clay

tofu High-protein food made from curdled soybean milk

tropical Very hot and humid

UNESCO United Nations Educational, Scientific, and Cultural Organization

World Heritage site Important historic site as recognized by UNESCO

Index